Cat

Laws, Practices

26 Questions and Answers

Daniel L. Lowery, C.SS.R.

LIGUORI
PUBLICATIONS

One Liguori Drive
Liguori, MO 63057-9999
(314) 464-2500

,

Imprimi Potest:
John F. Dowd, C.SS.R.
Provincial, St. Louis Province
The Redemptorists

Imprimatur:
+ Edward J. O'Donnell
Vicar General, Archdiocese of St. Louis

ISBN 0-89243-213-6

Copyright © 1984, Liguori Publications
Printed in U.S.A.

All rights reserved. No part of this booklet may be reproduced, stored in a retrieval system, or transmitted in any manner without the written permission of Liguori Publications.

Excerpts from the NEW CATHOLIC ENCYCLOPEDIA published by The Catholic University of America © 1967 have been used with permission.

Excerpts from VATICAN II: THE CONCILIAR AND POSTCONCILIAR DOCUMENTS, edited by Austin Flannery, O.P., copyright © 1975, Costello Publishing Company, Northport, NY, are used by permission of the publisher. All rights reserved.

Excerpts from THE CODE OF CANON LAW, English translation © 1983, The Canon Law Society Trust, published by Collins Liturgical Publications, London, England, have been used by permission. THE CODE OF CANON LAW is distributed in the U.S.A. by William B. Eerdmans Publishing Co., and in Canada by Publications Service, Canadian Conference of Catholic Bishops.

Scripture texts used in this work are taken from the NEW AMERICAN BIBLE, copyright © 1970 by the Confraternity of Christian Doctrine, Washington, D.C., and are used by permission of copyright owner. All rights reserved.

Excerpts from the English translation of RITE OF PENANCE © 1974, International Committee on English in the Liturgy, Inc. (ICEL); excerpts from the English translation of PASTORAL CARE OF THE SICK: RITES OF ANOINTING AND VIATICUM © 1982, ICEL. All rights reserved.

Excerpts from THE CHALLENGE OF PEACE: GOD'S PROMISE AND OUR RESPONSE copyright © 1983 and TO LIVE IN CHRIST JESUS copyright © 1976, Publications Office, United States Catholic Conference, Washington, D.C., are used by permission. All rights reserved.

Dedicated with love to
my brothers and sisters
James
Wilfred
Bernard (deceased)
Patricia
Donald
Glennon
Joan

TABLE OF CONTENTS

FOREWORD

When I first studied moral theology, before the dawn of Vatican II, a popular approach to the subject was the case-method approach. The student would be presented with a case about a fictional Bertha or Titus (or sometimes Bertha and Titus together!) and be asked to apply the general principles of Christian morality or canon law to this particular case. It was a way of getting the student out of the clouds of abstract principles down to the nitty-gritty where people live and act. Many business and medical courses still use the case-method approach.

In moral theology, however, this casuistic method (as it was called) got a bad name. It was accused of, and to some extent guilty of, contributing to hairsplitting Phariseeism and non-Gospel legalism in the Church. The method has been more or less abandoned in the past twenty years.

Whatever its faults, however, it did tend to call for the application of Gospel principles to the real and complex circumstances of peoples' lives. Difficult questions do arise in forming one's Christian conscience and in applying the law of the Church. I believe that these questions are worthy of careful attention.

The questions included in this booklet are from real people and arise from real situations. They deserve, it seems to me, respectful responses. In selecting these questions I have tried to choose those that seemed to have some relevance for others as well as for the individual persons who asked them. In other words, this or that question seemed to me to be the kind of question that other Catholics might also ask.

In responding to them, I have avoided a yes/no, right/wrong approach. I have also tried to avoid the unsavory legalism mentioned above. I have tried to raise up for explicit consideration a relevant teaching of the Church (especially from the documents of Vatican II) or an explanation of the Church's law. (There are, for example, some twenty references in these pages to the new Code of Canon Law promulgated by Pope John Paul II in 1983.)

The responses to these questions represent my small contribution to the "continuing education and formation" required of every Catholic. I am well aware that an intellectual understanding of Catholic teaching is only a part of one's total formation of conscience and total moral response to the Lord. But it *is* a part and worthy of our attention.

Several of these pieces appeared, in somewhat different form, in the *Liguorian*. I thank Norman Muckerman, C.SS.R., editor of the *Liguorian,* for permission to include them here. Several other pieces appeared first in the popular Dear Padre Sunday bulletin. I thank Richard Boever, C.SS.R., editor of that bulletin, for permission to reprint them in this booklet.

A special word of thanks is due to Christopher Farrell, C.SS.R., editor-in-chief of Liguori Publications' book department, for his kind and expert editing of this material; and to Roger Marchand for a number of valuable suggestions.

Most of all, I thank all those who have entrusted their questions to me. It was their hope, I'm sure, that their questions would be treated respectfully and answered with some measure of competence. I hope that my answers in this booklet have shown respect for the questions and have provided at least a glimmer of light for those who submitted them.

— Daniel L. Lowery, C.SS.R.

I. QUESTIONS ABOUT SIN, GUILT, RECONCILIATION

What Is a Serious Sin?
How Do I Get Rid of Guilt Feelings?
What Is Scrupulosity?
The Sacrament of Penance:
  How Can I Get More Out of It?

WHAT IS A SERIOUS SIN?

Q. For years I have been troubled about going to confession. The main trouble is in determining what is or is not a serious or mortal sin. I was once told that there are just four serious sins. Is this true, and if so, what would they be?

A. You should not feel that you are alone in this difficulty. It is certainly not always easy to determine what is or is not a serious sin. I don't believe, however, that a mathematical approach to sin is very helpful.

It is indeed sometimes alleged that only four specific sins were confessed in the early Church: namely, apostasy, blasphemy, homicide, and adultery. The historical evidence for this assertion, however, is by no means clear. In fact, some Church historians flatly deny that it is true.

Whatever be the case, the present teaching of the Church concerning the confession of sins quite clearly embraces more. That teaching is summarized in the new Code of Canon Law: ''The faithful are bound to confess, in kind and in number, all grave sins committed after baptism, of which after careful examination of conscience they are aware, which have not yet been directly pardoned by the keys of the Church, and which have not been confessed in an individual confession'' (Canon 988, §1).

The question of how to determine what is or is not a serious sin is not a new one. In the course of time it gave rise to a practical method of discernment, a pastoral aid for the ordinary person. This method concentrates on the so-called *conditions* for serious sin. Before a person is guilty of serious sin, three conditions must be verified: (1) the matter must be grave or serious; (2) there must be sufficient reflection; and (3) there must be full consent of the will.

I am aware that some theologians and pastors do not favor this approach. They seem to think that it does not plumb the depths of what sin really is, that it leads to too many "automatic" decisions about serious sin, that it is too cut and dried. Nonetheless, I personally believe that the traditional approach, when prudently used, is still a practical help to most Christians.

Though I cannot here provide an in-depth analysis of these conditions, I would like to offer the following insights with the hope that they may shed light on your dilemma. (I have treated some of these questions at greater length in chapters two and three of my book, *Following Christ: A Handbook of Catholic Moral Teaching,* available from Liguori Publications, Box 060, Liguori, MO 63057.)

First, the matter must be grave or serious. In ordinary human relationships, we can readily see that there are certain kinds of actions that place only a slight strain on the relationship while there are others that tend to destroy the relationship. In a similar way, the Scriptures and the teaching of the Church indicate that certain kinds of human actions are of greater moral significance than others and bring about greater harm in our relationship with God and other people. They are the kinds of actions that engage us in a serious way.

Saint Paul gives a number of examples of what he considers

serious matter when he contrasts the works of the flesh (sin) and the works of the spirit (virtue). He doesn't hesitate to spell out the kinds of actions he is talking about: "Do not deceive yourselves: no fornicators, idolaters, or adulterers, no sexual perverts, thieves, misers, or drunkards, no slanderers or robbers will inherit God's kingdom" (1 Corinthians 6:9-10. See also Galatians 5:19-21). Over the centuries the Church has certainly named other kinds of actions that involve serious matter. For example, obliteration bombing, artificial contraception, racial discrimination.

Second, there must be sufficient reflection. This is sometimes referred to as "full advertence." It implies that a person is clearly aware of the seriousness of the action he or she is contemplating and the choice he or she is making. This advertence surely implies the ability to appreciate certain basic moral values, such as love, justice, honesty, truth. Thus, it is doubtful that a child is capable of committing a serious sin. Persons in a condition of half-sleep or "twilight fantasy" would hardly be capable of sufficient reflection.

Third, there must be full consent of the will. This most important condition means that a person freely chooses to do what he or she knows is seriously wrong even though he or she could stop from doing it. Unfortunately, a number of things — for example, drugs, external force, inner compulsions — can either destroy or diminish human freedom. Without freedom, serious sin is not possible. It remains true, however, that a person may bear moral responsibility for the condition which diminished his or her freedom.

I suggest that a reasonable application of these three conditions to your own behavior will help you in determining what is and what is not a serious sin. At the same time, it seems appropriate to remind you that in preparing for the confession of your sins you are not expected to have mathematical certitude. Nor are you expected to be able to label every sin perfectly. All that is required is a simple and sincere statement of your sins as you see them. Leave the rest in the merciful hands of the Lord!

HOW DO I GET RID OF GUILT FEELINGS?

Q. I've lived with guilt most of my life. I've been in a living hell of guilt for a long time. I am so tired of feeling guilty for things that really weren't my fault. I want to get out of this hell and ignore the guilt feelings, but don't know how.

A. Guilt is a common but complex human experience. A clearer analysis of it may be of some help to you. First of all it is important, I believe, to distinguish between "true guilt" and "false guilt" or "real guilt" and "neurotic guilt."

According to Catholic theology, true or real guilt is a state or condition that follows upon a deliberate, personal, willful transgression of the law of God. In other words, *guilt follows upon sin*.

Awareness of guilt, in its turn, gives rise to *guilt feelings*; that is, feelings of inner unrest or discomfort of conscience that seek to be relieved. Ideally, guilt feelings urge a person to make amends so that the feelings can be erased or relieved.

We see here the familiar pattern of Christian Penance: consciousness that I have sinned, that I have fallen short of the mark; honest admission of this sin by confession; true sorrow for it, including a willingness to make restitution; the forgiveness of God through the sign of absolution given by the priest who represents the community of the Church; an experience of reconciliation, a feeling of relief!

From this brief description it's clear that such true guilt, rooted in reality, is spiritually wholesome. It follows upon a true moral disorder (sin), and it leads to repentance and forgiveness. The whole process is a gift of God!

False or neurotic guilt, on the other hand, arises not from a deliberate, personal, willful transgression of the law of God but, rather, from a vague, generalized, compulsive conviction that "I must have sinned," "I always do the wrong thing," "I am no good."

False guilt gives rise to nonstop and agonizing guilt feelings.

You express it well: "I've been in a living hell of guilt for a long time." Yet, these guilt feelings inspire one not to positive amendment and reconciliation but to progressive anxiety and unrest. Again, you express the feeling well: "I am tired of feeling guilty for things that were really not my fault."

The severity of false guilt feelings will vary, of course, from person to person. In some cases, only prolonged professional counseling can begin to alleviate the pain. In less severe cases, certain positive attitudes and actions can be of help. I would suggest the following:

1. *A mature and objective formation of conscience*. It may seem odd to emphasize this, but it is true that neurotic guilt can stem from an ill-formed conscience, especially one based on excessively rigid principles imposed in childhood. It is liberating, therefore, to try to form one's conscience in conformity to the teaching of Christ and the Church — and to measure guilt only according to that standard.

2. *A deepening of the virtue of hope and trust*. Anything the guilt-ridden person can do to change his or her image of God — from that of a stern and unrelenting Judge to that of a loving and forgiving Father — is a big step in the right direction. In prayer, try to "let go and let God," to "cast your cares upon the Lord."

3. *An effort to "act against" guilt feelings*. This amounts to ignoring them, dismissing them, brushing them off, not allowing them to dictate one's behavior. Every victory is a giant stride toward true moral freedom and maturity.

I hope that these suggestions are of help to you in escaping the hell of false guilt.

WHAT IS SCRUPULOSITY?

Q. A friend of mine is a very fearful and worrisome kind of person. Her confessor told her that she suffers from scrupulosity. I have heard this term before, but its meaning is not clear to me. I would appreciate an explanation.

A. For centuries theologians, as well as psychologists, have grappled with the condition of scrupulosity. There are a number of different explanations of what it is, where it comes from, and how to deal with it. The following explanation by Cyril Harney, O.P., will give you a good basic grasp of what theologians mean by scrupulosity.

The word *scrupulus* is a Latin word meaning a small sharp stone. "The scrupulous person's life journey has been aptly likened to that of a traveler whose pebble-filled shoes make every step painful and hesitant. Scruples render one incapable of making with finality the daily decisions of life. . . . It [scrupulosity] causes ordinary, everyday questions to be viewed as impenetrable and insoluble. Decisions require a disproportionate amount of time and energy, and are always accompanied by feelings of guilt and doubt. Never at peace, the mind compulsively reexamines and reevaluates every aspect of a matter about which scruples center. With increasing doubts and mounting fear the mind is so blinded and confused that volitional activity becomes difficult or impossible. The will is unable to act without immediately reacting against its previous decision. There is a more or less constant, unreasonable, and morbid fear of sin, error, and guilt" (*New Catholic Encyclopedia*).

It is evident, then, that scrupulosity is a religious-moral-psychological state of anxiety, fear, and indecision. It manifests itself in many ways. The scrupulous person often repeats prayers again and again because he or she cannot get them "right." Not surprisingly, the sacrament of Penance, with its confession of sins, is often a torture to the scrupulous person. He or she is never satisfied that sins have been confessed exactly; there is a constant desire to make a general confession "one more time." Every passing sexual thought is considered a mortal sin. Normal feelings of impatience or anger are blown out of proportion. The scrupulous person experiences sin and guilt almost all the time.

Your friend is fortunate that she has a confessor who has diagnosed the state of her soul. While there does not seem to be a cure for scrupulosity, there are helpful ways of dealing with it. From a spiritual viewpoint, according to the masters of the spiritual life, it is very important that a scrupulous person have one confessor and that he or she be determined to abide by the decisions of that confessor. To flit from one confessor to another is disastrous for the scrupulous person. It is also helpful for the scrupulous person to "act against" his or her fears; for example, to receive Holy Communion at Mass, despite the worry that he or she may have committed a serious sin.

I should also mention a self-help organization called Scrupulous Anonymous. The late Father Thomas Tobin, a Redemptorist priest and professional counselor, founded this organization in 1964. Its purpose is to provide self-help to those who suffer from scrupulosity. This is done through a four-page monthly bulletin, edited by the priest director. The bulletin offers tips and suggestions from a wide variety of sources. At the present time there are approximately seven thousand members enrolled in Scrupulous Anonymous. They are of all ages and from all walks of life. The bulletin is sent each month free of charge. The only condition for membership is that a person request it for himself or herself. (Experience has taught us it is unwise to send the bulletin to a wife at the request of her husband, to a mother at the request of her daughter, to a neighbor at the request of a neighbor!) The address is: Department S.A., Liguori, MO 63057.

THE SACRAMENT OF PENANCE:
HOW CAN I GET MORE OUT OF IT?

Q. According to our Catholic newspaper, Pope John Paul II is really emphasizing confession for Catholics. I go to confession on a regular basis, yet I find that I don't get much out of this sacrament and don't make much spiritual progress. I'm definitely in a rut. I must be doing something wrong! Do you have any suggestions for me?

A. I'm sure you are not the only Catholic who has these feelings. Perhaps the following suggestions — ways of approaching this sacrament — will help you out of the rut.

First, be prayerful. It may seem odd that I would stress this, but it's easy enough for us to bounce in and bounce out of the confessional without giving much attention to prayer or reflection. The sacrament of Penance is a celebration of the generous mercy of our loving Father, made manifest in the death and Resurrection of his Son, Jesus. This sacrament is "a mystery of faith" (as are all the sacraments), a mystery best approached on our knees, in an atmosphere of prayer. The Church suggests that there be prayer *before* ("a prayer for genuine confidence in the mercy of God"), *during* ("a prayer for God's pardon"), and *after* ("praising the mercy of God and giving him thanks"). In addition, the Church encourages some reflection on the Word of God as a fitting preparation for this sacrament. Such preparation is, I believe, the best safeguard against "getting in a rut," as you express it.

Second, be personal. Many Catholics have a "regular confessor," that is, a priest to whom they ordinarily confess. They know the confessor and he knows them. There is great spiritual value in such a relationship. If you do not have such a confessor, I encourage you to look for one. When no such relationship exists, however, the penitent should at least take a few moments to reveal some personal information about himself or herself; for example, a few words about one's age and state in life, one's major responsibilities, one's helps and hindrances in leading a Christian life. The personal dimensions of this sacrament are extremely important. There is always the danger of thinking of it as a cold and inhuman vending machine (drop in the coins of confession and contrition and out pops forgiveness) rather than a warm and personal encounter between Christ and the Christian, an encounter like that between Jesus and the Samaritan woman at the well. Whatever you can do to emphasize the essential personalism of this sacrament will be worth the effort.

Third, be penitent. This may seem too obvious to deserve

mention; yet, because we are human and because we tend to be more comfortable with externals than with internals, there is a temptation to place too much emphasis on the confession of sins and not enough on the deeper demands of this sacrament. To be sure, the confession of our sins is an important part of this sacrament; in the case of grave sins it is an absolute requirement. "To obtain the saving remedy of the sacrament of penance, according to the plan of our merciful God, the faithful must confess to a priest each and every grave sin which they remember upon examination of their conscience" (Rite of Penance, 1973, #7a). In the case of light or venial sins, it seems wise to focus on those that more clearly manifest the roots of selfishness in one's life. Yet preoccupation with the confession itself should not be allowed to divert us from the deeper demands of true penitence, real contrition, interior conversion. This sacrament is meant to touch the deep recesses of our hearts, not merely our external behavior.

Finally, be prophetic. That is, be an effective witness to the realities of this sacrament. The reconciled sinner tries to become a prophetic witness of the merciful and reconciling love of God. The Christian who has experienced the forgiving and healing love of Christ should be better able to love others as brothers and sisters and to forgive them in the name of Christ. Walter Burghardt, S.J., entitled one of his Lenten homilies "For Your Penance, Look Redeemed." Having experienced the sacrament of Penance with its effect of reconciliation, we should look and talk and act redeemed! In the long run, that may be the best standard against which to judge your use of this sacrament: if the power of sacrament flows into your daily life, then you're not really in a rut!

II. QUESTIONS ABOUT CATHOLIC BELIEFS, LITURGY, PRACTICES

How Can Swearing Be Justified?
Is It All Right to Miss Sunday Mass
  "Once in a While"?
Sunday Mass: Can a Weekday Take Its Place?
Is There Still an Easter Duty?
Communion in the Hand: Is There a Problem?
May Communion Be Received
  More Than Once a Day?
Are Catholics Allowed to Be Cremated?
The Sacrament of Anointing: Who May Receive It?

HOW CAN SWEARING BE JUSTIFIED?

Q. The Bible says that it is forbidden to swear. I am always hearing people say that they swear to one thing or another. Also, people are required to swear in court. Recently I was asked to swear as to the facts in a hearing. I refused to do so. Is it wrong to swear? What does the Bible mean by that law?

A. Your letter brings up an important and difficult moral topic. Important because it raises questions about the conduct of Christians in secular society. Difficult because it involves the interpretation of the Bible by the Christian community. I will try to throw some light on the major points at issue in this disputed matter.

But first, since the term "swear" is used in different ways by different people, let's agree on how we are using it here. By swearing we mean calling on the name of God to witness the truth of a statement or promise. Thus the term "swear" is synonymous with "taking an oath."

What does the Bible say about swearing? The Old Testament seems not to condemn it absolutely but, rather, to condemn *false* swearing. For example, "The LORD, your God, shall you fear; him shall you serve, and by his name shall you swear" (Deuteronomy 6:13). "You shall not swear falsely by my name, thus profaning the name of your God" (Leviticus 19:12). In the New Testament, Saint Paul himself quite often takes an oath, calling God to witness the truth of what he has written. For example, "I declare before God that what I have just written is true" (Galatians 1:20. See also Romans 1:9; 2 Corinthians 1:23; 1 Thessalonians 2:5).

But the key text of the New Testament, and I'm sure it's the one you refer to in your letter, is this: "You have heard the commandment imposed on your forefathers, 'Do not take a false oath. . . . ' What I tell you is: do not swear at all. Do not swear by heaven (it is God's throne), nor by the earth (it is his footstool), nor by Jerusalem (it is the city of the great King); do not swear by your head (you cannot make a single hair white or black). Say, 'Yes' when you mean 'Yes' and 'No' when you mean 'No.' Anything beyond that is from the evil one" (Matthew 5:33-37. See also James 5:12).

The basic question about this saying of Jesus is: Must it be understood *literally?* In the course of Christian history, right up to our own day, there have been two different responses to that question.

The first — and by far the more common — may be stated this way: No, this text is not to be understood literally. In the context of the Sermon on the Mount where it occurs, it is a call to absolute honesty and simplicity of speech. It describes the ideal society in which each person should be able to trust the word of others and thus render oaths unnecessary. In the present state of social relationships, however, oaths may be used, but not for light or trivial reasons, and only in support of the truth. It would be wrong to call on God's name to support a lie (perjury) or for other immoral purposes.

The second response may be described thus: The words of Jesus should be taken literally. They should not be watered down to a mere vague ideal. The Christian is expected to challenge the unreformed society in which he or she lives, not to go along with its customs. It is morally wrong to swear.

It is clear that Catholic moral theology and the Code of Canon Law have accepted the first response outlined above: namely, that God's name may be invoked when necessary or very useful to confirm the truth. Thus, in the new Code of Canon Law, we read: "An oath is the invocation of the divine Name as witness to the truth. It cannot be taken except in truth, judgement and justice" (Canon 1199, §1). While swearing is sometimes justified, at all times reverence for God's name, simplicity of speech, and total honesty should be hallmarks of the Christian's behavior.

IS IT ALL RIGHT TO MISS SUNDAY MASS "ONCE IN A WHILE"?

Q. My neighbor told me that she read in a Catholic magazine that a Catholic commits no sin by missing Mass on Sunday once in a while, even though there is no good reason for it. I have never heard this before. Is it true?

A. I may have heard it before, but it does not appear true to me. It seems to me to be a very legalistic approach to the Sunday Mass obligation and the fundamental reason for it.

The celebration of the Eucharist is the chief element in the Catholic Christian's observance of the Lord's Day. The Church is the family of God. At Sunday Mass the family gathers together around the table of the Lord to celebrate and take part in the Lord's sacrificial banquet.

The Eucharist is the very heart of Catholic worship. The new

Code of Canon Law beautifully summarizes the ancient faith of the Church when it says: ''The eucharistic Sacrifice, the memorial of the death and resurrection of the Lord, in which the Sacrifice of the Cross is forever perpetuated, is the summit and the source of all worship and christian life. By means of it the unity of God's people is signified and brought about, and the building up of the body of Christ is perfected. The other sacraments and all the apostolic works of Christ are bound up with, and directed to, the blessed Eucharist'' (Canon 897).

The obligation to attend Mass on Sunday really flows from our faith in this great mystery of the Eucharist. I like to think that the law of the Church (that Catholics are obliged to attend Mass on Sunday) is in reality a reminder of an intrinsic religious obligation rather than the cause of one. That is to say, the obligation arises out of our faith conviction about the meaning of Sunday and the meaning of the Eucharist. I like the way Vatican II expresses the obligation: ''On this day [Sunday] Christ's faithful are bound to come together into one place. They should listen to the word of God and take part in the Eucharist, thus calling to mind the passion, resurrection, and glory of the Lord Jesus, and giving thanks to God who 'has begotten them again through the resurrection of Christ from the dead, unto a living hope' (1 Peter 1:3)'' (*The Sacred Liturgy,* 106).

For centuries the Church has had an explicit law obliging Catholics to assist at Mass on Sundays. That law is stated again in the new Code of Canon Law promulgated by Pope John Paul II in 1983 (see Canon 1243). The obligation is certainly considered a serious one. Deliberately to miss Mass without a sufficient reason is considered a grave (not light) transgression of the law of the Church. At the same time, the law of the Church, in this case as in others, is not unreasonable. Proportionately serious reasons can excuse a person from attendance at Sunday Mass: for example, sickness, demands of charity (such as taking care of an ill family member), occupation, severe weather, a great distance from the church, and the like.

To return to your question, it makes no sense to me to say that "a Catholic commits no sin by missing Mass on Sunday once in a while, even though there is no good reason for it." To be sure, it is not for me to judge when a particular individual commits a sin. But such a casual and casuistic approach to the Sunday Mass obligation would lead me to believe that the author of the article either does not have a full understanding of the inner reason for the Church's law or does not have a mature faith appreciation for the Eucharist itself. All in all, I consider it bad advice.

SUNDAY MASS: CAN A WEEKDAY TAKE ITS PLACE?

Q. In reference to the Sunday Mass obligation, about which you have written, my wife and I have discussed this matter at length. We have a "theory" which we practice from time to time, especially during vacation. The nub of our theory is that we don't believe it makes much difference if we attend Mass on Sunday as such. Why not on Monday or Thursday? Sometimes a more peaceful, more quiet, less crowded atmosphere helps us in drawing closer to the Lord, and isn't that the whole point? Do you agree with our point of view?

A. No, I do not agree with your point of view. Without in any way questioning your personal piety or sincerity, I believe that your theory is quite inadequate. I say this for the following reasons.

First, in the Christian view of life Sunday is *not* like Monday or Thursday. Sunday is special. It is a holy day, a feast day. In the words of the new Code of Canon Law: "The Lord's Day, on which the paschal mystery is celebrated, is by apostolic tradition to be observed in the universal Church as the primary holyday of obligation" (Canon 1246, §1). This canon simply reflects the teaching of Vatican II: "The Lord's Day is the original feast day, and it should be proposed to the faithful and taught to them so that it may become in fact a day of joy and freedom from work'' (*The Sacred Liturgy,* 106).

Second, your viewpoint exhibits a common misunderstanding about the Sunday Eucharistic liturgy. You do not seem to understand that this is not a private devotion; it is a family celebration, a celebration of the community. Its main purpose is not peace and quiet but the joyful celebration of faith by the People of God. There is, to be sure, a great value in silent, reflective prayer — there are times and places for silent prayer in the liturgy itself — but this is not the primary focus of the Sunday liturgy. Vatican II emphasized this when it said: ''Liturgical services are not private functions but are celebrations of the Church which is 'the sacrament of unity,' namely, 'the holy people united and arranged under their bishops.'

''Therefore, liturgical services pertain to the whole Body of the Church. . . . It must be emphasized that rites which are meant to be celebrated in common, with the faithful present and actively participating, should as far as possible be celebrated in that way rather than by an individual and quasi-privately.

''This applies with special force to the celebration of Mass. . . . '' (*The Sacred Liturgy,* 26-27).

Much of the dissatisfaction that some Catholics experienced with the revised liturgy of Vatican II was due, I believe, to their early formation. That formation — and it was mine as well — did not place very much emphasis on the community. It tended to be a highly individualistic formation. It did not make clear that God ''willed to make men holy and save them, not as individuals without any bond or link between them, but rather to make them into a people who might acknowledge him and serve him in holiness'' (*The Church,* 9). Not understanding that the liturgy is the prayerful celebration of the People of God, as a people, some Catholics tended to resent the intrusion into their world of private prayer. Some still do.

Without doubt, there have been abuses in the liturgy — too much noise, too many words, too many ''handouts'' — and I certainly do not defend them. But the solution is not to substitute

Thursday for Sunday in order to find a more quiet and peaceful atmosphere. I hope you and your wife will rethink your theory. You should be there on Sunday with the rest of the family! You need the community, and the community needs you.

IS THERE STILL AN EASTER DUTY?

Q. Would you please explain the Easter duty? We seldom hear it mentioned anymore. Is it still an obligation?

A. The Easter duty refers to the law of the Church that obliges the members of the Church to receive Holy Communion during the Easter (Paschal) season. In this context the Easter season is understood to extend from the first Sunday of Lent until Trinity Sunday. The new Code of Canon Law adds that "for a just cause" the Easter duty may be fulfilled at another time of the year. Here is the complete text of the new Code: "Once admitted to the blessed Eucharist, each of the faithful is obliged to receive holy communion at least once a year. This precept must be fulfilled during paschal time, unless for a good reason it is fulfilled at another time during the year" (Canon 920, §1 and §2).

A question that frequently arises in this context is: What about the sacrament of Penance in relation to the Easter duty?

Strictly speaking, the law does not require that one receive the sacrament of Penance as an essential part of the Easter duty. The sacrament of Penance is required only if one is conscious of an unconfessed grave sin. In a canon different from the one that describes the Easter duty, the following obligation is stated: "All the faithful who have reached the age of discretion are bound faithfully to confess their grave sins at least once a year" (Canon 989). It follows that if one is not conscious of grave sin, one is not obliged to confess once a year.

In calling attention to these canons, I do not intend to downplay the confession of venial sins in the sacrament of Penance. This is highly recommended by the Church. (See Canon 988, §2.) My intention is to clarify the thinking of those people who will not receive Communion unless they have first confessed, even if they are not conscious of grave sin. They should know that the law of the Church does not prohibit them from receiving Holy Communion.

Personally, I am not too surprised that we seldom hear about the Easter duty these days. After all, this involves the bare minimum for a Catholic. Surely most active Catholics receive Holy Communion more than once a year. I doubt that inactive Catholics would be greatly influenced by having this obligation spelled out for them. My pastoral experience indicates that the person who receives the Eucharist only once a year — unless there are very special reasons involved — will not be an active Catholic very long!

COMMUNION IN THE HAND: IS THERE A PROBLEM?

Q. I am having difficulty with Communion in the hand. While I realize that the more customary option of receiving the Holy Eucharist on the tongue is still available, I would like to begin receiving in the hand. However, I perceive the hands as instruments used in committing sin (such as theft, uncharitable gestures, impure acts) and therefore feel it may be somewhat blasphemous to receive the Eucharist in the hands. Perhaps you can offer some advice that will help clarify my thinking.

A. It strikes me that the first difficulty with your thinking on this matter is that it is *sin-dominated*. Why put the emphasis on sin? If one wanted to think in this way, one could also make a case that the tongue is an instrument for committing sin, such as perjury, slander, obscenity. Why not accentuate the positive? After all, the tongue and the hand may also be instruments of prayer, kindness, justice.

Communion in the hand, like so many other liturgical changes, has become a red flag for some Catholics. To me this is unfortunate; it creates tension and stress where none should exist. A simple review of the history of the Church shows that for the first nine hundred years of her existence Communion in the hand was the normal practice. During the second half of her existence (the past thousand years), Communion on the tongue was the customary practice. The Church (through the National Conference of Catholic Bishops) now offers a choice to the individual communicant. Why should that become a matter of controversy? Why do some people feel called upon to be "holier than the Church" and condemn one practice or the other?

It seems to me that one should concentrate not so much on the external manner in which one receives the Eucharist (on the tongue or in the hand) but, rather, on the spirit of reverence which one brings to this great sacrament. Because regular reception of this sacrament is a "natural" part of Catholic life, it is easy to fall into a casual and loose attitude toward it. In this case familiarity breeds carelessness. Parents should gently remind children from time to time about their comportment in approaching the Eucharist. We adults need similar reminders. The new Code of Canon Law simply but clearly describes what our attitude should be: "Christ's faithful are to hold the blessed Eucharist in the highest honour. They should take an active part in the celebration of the most august Sacrifice of the Mass; they should receive the sacrament with great devotion and frequently, and should reverence it with the greatest adoration" (Canon 898).

Concerning your present dilemma, I suggest that you feel perfectly free to receive Communion either on the tongue or in the hand. As you think about Communion in the hand, try to set aside the concentration on sin and reflect rather on the following passage taken from a fourth century catechetical instruction. It deftly describes the beautiful symbolism of Communion in the hand: "When you approach Communion do not come with your hands outstretched or with your fingers open, but make your one hand a throne for the other, which is to receive the King. With your hand hollowed receive the Body of Christ and answer Amen!"

MAY COMMUNION BE RECEIVED MORE THAN
ONCE A DAY?

Q. During Lent I sometimes have the opportunity to attend Mass twice on the same day: for example, in the morning when I take my son to school and in the early evening at a downtown church near my office. When this happens I feel very privileged. But I've been told that I may receive Holy Communion only once a day. I do not understand why this is so. I wish I could receive at each Mass.

A. The new Code of Canon Law (1983) has granted your wish! "One who has received the blessed Eucharist may receive it again on the same day only within a eucharistic celebration in which that person participates . . . " (Canon 917). I believe that many priests and people are happy about this change in the Church's law.

At the same time, the reason for the former law (that a person should receive Holy Communion only once a day) was important. The reason was to safeguard against the mentality that says, "If one Communion is good, two or three or four must be better." Such a mentality borders on the superstitious, and tends to trivialize the real meaning of the Eucharist.

It is clear that the new law does not wish to encourage "counting" Communions. Rather, its purpose is to promote full participation in every Eucharistic liturgy in which one participates. We should be thankful for this new law but not forget the reason for the old!

ARE CATHOLICS ALLOWED TO BE CREMATED?

Q. May a practicing Catholic be cremated without any special reasons demanded by the Church for cremation? We're asking for an answer because we attended a mission and the priest speaker said, "The Catholic Church permits cremation and I intend to be cremated." But my husband's brother is a priest and he said, "That is not accurate. One has to have a legitimate reason for cremation." Since we are changing our wills and intend to specify "cremation," please inform us.

A. It is noteworthy how often this question of cremation arises. That is due, no doubt, to the way most middle-aged-and-over Catholics were taught. When I was young, cremation was certainly considered to be absolutely forbidden for Catholics. The old Canon Law was quite clear: "The bodies of the faithful must be buried; their cremation is reprobated" (Canon 1203).

In July 1963, however, the Church issued a decree on cremation. This decree modified the law cited above. The new decree emphasized the following points:

1. The Church prefers the traditional rite of Christian burial, and in ordinary circumstances the faithful should choose this rite.

2. The law against cremation must be observed "in those cases where it is evident that cremation was requested as a denial of Christian belief or in a sectarian spirit or out of hatred for the Catholic religion."

3. In other cases, however, cremation may be requested if there is a good reason for the request.

4. The rites of Christian burial are to be performed for the deceased person but not at the place of cremation.

What is a "good reason" for the request? Theologians suggest that cremation is justified if it is the custom of one's country, if there is danger of disease, if there is a lack of cemetery space, if the cost of burial is unreasonably expensive, and other similar reasons of a personal, hygienic, or financial nature.

From this you can see that the Church, while preferring burial, does permit cremation, as the missionary said; but there should be a legitimate reason, as your husband's brother said. In other words, both of them were correct.

The basic thrust of this 1963 decree is now incorporated in the new Canon Law of 1983. Interestingly enough, however, there is no mention of the need for a good reason. The canon says simply: "The Church earnestly recommends that the pious custom of burial be retained; but it does not forbid cremation, unless this is chosen for reasons which are contrary to christian teaching" (Canon 1176, §3).

From pastoral experience, I would suggest that one who is planning cremation should discuss this with one's loved ones so as to avoid unnecessary shock or dismay. I would further suggest that one consult with one's pastor concerning one's plans and concerning the details of the rites to be performed.

THE SACRAMENT OF ANOINTING: WHO MAY RECEIVE IT?

Q. One Sunday afternoon I attended a beautiful ceremony in my sister's parish church. It was a special Mass which also included the Anointing of the Sick. Those who were to be anointed wore big name tags. There were several people in wheelchairs and a number of really elderly people. But the priest also anointed a teenage boy, a woman who looked to be about forty, and some older people who seemed to me to be in good health. I was so excited by the ceremony that I wanted to be anointed! Who is allowed to receive this sacrament?

A. Your question is a good one. It provides me an opportunity to review the Church's guidelines concerning one of the great Christian sacraments.

In 1972, Pope Paul VI issued an apostolic constitution (a formal document) called: "Rite of Anointing and Pastoral Care of the Sick." At the same time he approved for use in the whole Church a revised Rite of Anointing. His purpose was to fulfill the desire of Vatican II that the real meaning of this sacrament be made as clear and visible as possible to the eyes of modern Catholics.

The Rite of Anointing addresses itself quite directly to your question. In speaking of the ''subject'' of this sacrament, it tells us who can and should receive this sacrament. The Rite states the following six principles:

1. ''The Letter of James states that the sick are to be anointed in order to raise them up and save them. Great care and concern should be taken to see that those of the faithful whose health is seriously impaired by sickness or old age receive this sacrament.'' Then, as if expecting that the question of how dangerous is dangerous or how sick is sick might arise, the Rite offers this common sense advice: ''A prudent or reasonably sure judgment, without scruple, is sufficient for deciding on the seriousness of an illness; if necessary a doctor may be consulted.''

2. ''The sacrament may be repeated if the sick person recovers after being anointed and then again falls ill or if during the same illness the person's condition becomes more serious.''

3. ''A sick person may be anointed before surgery whenever a serious illness is the reason for the surgery.''

4. ''Elderly people may be anointed if they have become notably weakened even though no serious illness is present.'' The Rite gives no specific age as constituting ''elderly people.'' A very common interpretation is that those who are over 65 may be anointed.

5. ''Sick children may be anointed if they have sufficient use of reason to be strengthened by this sacrament.''

6. ''The sacrament of anointing may be conferred upon sick people who, although they have lost consciousness or the use of reason, would, as Christian believers, probably have asked for it were they in control of their faculties.'' (The Rite of Anointing and Pastoral Care of the Sick, #8, 9, 10, 11, 12, 14)

You can see that these principles cover most of the cases you were wondering about. Thus, though the teenage boy may have looked healthy, he was no doubt suffering from some serious illness. The woman of forty may have been facing serious surgery. The older people who seemed in good health may have been feeling the effects of old age and approached the sacrament for strength and courage. All of these are good reasons for receiving the sacrament.

By way of conclusion, let me share with you a beautiful statement which sums up the faith of the Church on the sacrament of anointing: ''This sacrament gives the grace of the Holy Spirit to those who are sick: by this grace the whole person is helped and saved, sustained by trust in God, and strengthened against the temptations of the Evil One and against anxiety over death. Thus the sick person is able not only to bear suffering bravely, but also to fight against it. A return to physical health may follow the reception of this sacrament if it will be beneficial to the sick person's salvation. If necessary, the sacrament also provides the sick person with the forgiveness of sins and the completion of Christian penance.'' (The Rite of Anointing and Pastoral Care of the Sick, #6)

What a wonderful sacrament the Lord has given us!

III. QUESTIONS ABOUT LIFE, JUSTICE, PEACE

WHY IS THERE SO MUCH ADDICTION TO DRUGS?

Q. I am forty-seven years old, happily married, and the father of three teenagers who, thank God, are very responsible kids. What really baffles me about our society is the widespread use of drugs. I am talking not so much about teenagers as about adults who are well-educated and financially well-off. Why do so many people become addicted to drugs?

A. Before offering a response to your question I would like to make a few basic distinctions about drugs. Experts define psychotropic (or psychoactive) drugs as chemicals that influence the mind and alter behavior, mood, and mental functioning.

These drugs may be used for two main purposes: (1) *therapeutic* — drugs used for the treatment of major mental illnesses such as schizophrenia or for the relief of depression, hyperactivity, anxiety, and the like; and (2) *non-therapeutic* — drugs used for personal enjoyment, self-transcendence, recreation, or a "high" of elation or pleasure. My remarks here refer to the non-therapeutic use of drugs.

There are many reasons given for the widespread use of drugs in our society and for the addiction that can so easily follow. Personally, I believe we are dealing with something very profound. When we speak of the forces that move people to addiction, we are speaking of the ancient scourges of the human spirit and the age-old hungers of the human heart.

There is a depth of wisdom in what Jesus said to Satan in the desert:

Scripture has it:

"Not on bread alone is man to live

but on every utterance that comes

    from the mouth of God" (Matthew 4:4).

Bread alone — material satisfaction and physical comfort — is not enough. The human person has deep spiritual and psychic needs: the need for love and belonging, for self-esteem and acceptance by others, for creativity and knowledge and beauty. And yes, a need for God! In the timeless words of Saint Augustine: "Our hearts are made for you, O God, and they are restless until they rest in you."

When these needs are not met — in one's family, one's relationships, one's job, one's culture — the human person goes searching for something that will fill the emptiness and ease the pain. The search goes down many byways: the piling up of material possessions and the conspicuous consumption of them, the achievement of power and the practice of aggressive behavior toward others, the use of drugs with the hope that they will bring the "high" one is searching for.

I believe that the fundamental spiritual needs of many people are not being met in our society. For many people there is no balance, no rhythm, no proportion to life. Frenzied activity crowds out the need for silence and contemplation. Material gain overrides spiritual integrity. Pleasure-at-any-price substitutes for happiness. Insecurity, guilt, fear, loneliness . . . often these are not faced but simply pushed under the rug of some passing satisfaction of the senses. Human beings try to live by bread alone!

I have known a number of people who have walked the long road back from addiction. One thing they know: Drugs did not and could not provide what they were looking for. Efforts to stay "high" are doomed to failure. Drugs may provide an escape, but they do not provide a solution. Drugs will never be able to give love, self-esteem, acceptance, and fulfillment. For those basics we will have to look elsewhere: to "every utterance that comes from the mouth of God."

IS BOXING IMMORAL?

Q. We had a big argument at work about boxing — whether it is really a sport, whether it is immoral, whether it should be banned. I often watch the fights on TV and enjoy them. Even I have to wonder at times if fights shouldn't be stopped sooner. I feel sorry about the way some boxers get beat up. Do you think boxing is immoral?

A. First, I would like to make a distinction between professional boxing and amateur, Olympic-style boxing. Some people do not agree with me, I know, but I think there's quite a difference. Amateur boxing seems to me to be a real sport. It can help a young person develop agility, coordination, and a confident feeling about using his body and its muscles in a positive way. It can be good training, I believe, in the "manly art of self-defense." The object is not to beat one's opponent unconscious but to score by deft blows. The "touch" is what counts, not the severity of the blow struck. At least that's my view!

Professional boxing is something else. Its whole purpose is to set up a situation in which the two boxers try to render each other unconscious or at least incapable of continuing the bout. Grace, agility, and skill do not matter very much. What really matters is to pound on one's opponent and to knock him unconscious.

It is hard for me to see how any Christian can consider professional boxing a truly human and moral activity. After all, the Christian recognizes that he or she is not the absolute master of his or her life and health but, rather, the steward or trustee of them. Good stewardship means that we should exercise responsibility in taking care of our physical health. Father Richard McCormick, S.J., a moral theologian who has written expertly on this topic, affirms that "theologians believe that when a man pounds another into helplessness, scars his face, smashes his nose, jars his brain and exposes it to lasting damage, or when he enters a contest when this could happen to him, he has surpassed the bounds of reasonable stewardship of the human person."

I would judge that, objectively speaking, it is immoral for a person to engage in professional boxing as it is now practiced. What, then, is to be said of those who promote it and watch it? Professional boxing is ultimately a money game. Most of the boxers seem to be men who are "up from poverty"; a disproportionate number are members of minorities. These men enter the ring because they hope to make big money. Television advertisers and arena patrons, in effect, pay their salaries. It is a chilling thought to realize that my money is being used to support two men who are trying to knock each other unconscious.

Many psychologists believe that the popularity of professional boxing is another facet of the peculiar fascination some people have for violence. Aggression is a powerful instinct. Many people who watch professional fights seem to be indulging in "socially acceptable aggressive behavior." They are not so much interested in sport and skill as they are in violence and bloodshed. It would be helpful, perhaps, if we stopped calling professional boxing a sport and called it by its correct name: legalized violence.

There have been many suggestions in recent years to make professional boxing more humane: for example, using heavier gloves and protective headgear, shortening the length of rounds and lengthening the period between rounds. But many boxers, promoters, and rabid fans oppose all such suggestions. One fan was quoted as saying, "They're trying to make it a sissy sport."

My response to that view would be: "No, they're just trying to make it a *sport,* rather than a spectacle where grown men pummel each other into unconsciousness."

In a world already grown too violent, we can do without professional boxing. At least that's my view!

DOES ABORTION BRING EXCOMMUNICATION?

Q. My understanding is that the Church imposes an automatic excommunication on anyone directly involved in an abortion, thus underlining the seriousness of this terrible sin. Could you please tell me how far down the line (advisor? janitor at a clinic?) this excommunication goes? Also, how is this excommunication reconciled with the idea that all sins can be forgiven?

A. Your letter indicates that you are a well-informed Catholic. The questions you have raised are important. I will try to respond to them in an adequate, but nontechnical, way.

First of all, you are correct about the Church's law. In the new Code of Canon Law (as in the old) a person who actually procures an abortion incurs an automatic excommunication (Canon 1398). I will touch on the meaning of excommunication below, but the basic reason for this severe penalty is that, in the moral teaching of the Church, abortion is considered "an unspeakable crime."

Second, in addition to the person who actually procures the abortion, accomplices also incur excommunication. Persons are considered accomplices "if, without their assistance, the crime would not have been committed" (Canon 1329, §2).

Who, then, would be liable to this excommunication? As a general rule:

— Catholics who obtain or perform an abortion,
— Catholics who persuade others to do so, and
— Catholics who deliberately assist in abortion procedures.

In this last category would certainly be included the attending physician and the health care personnel who assist in the abortion procedures. For this reason physicians, nurses, and others who work in hospitals that perform abortions should formally notify the hospital administrator that they are bound in conscience to refuse to participate in abortions.

Ordinarily, those who take general care of the patient before or after an abortion (for example, the nurse on duty) would not be included under the excommunication. Nor would persons who are only remotely concerned with medical procedures, such as a janitor or cook. (Since abortion is so taken for granted in our society, however, people in these positions may feel obliged in conscience to avoid any actions which appear to give approval to abortion.)

What is meant by an excommunication? An excommunication is a penalty imposed by the Church. By force of this penalty, as the new Code of Canon Law points out, "An excommunicated person is forbidden: (1) to have any ministerial part in the celebration of the Sacrifice of the Eucharist or in any other ceremonies of public worship; (2) to celebrate the sacraments or sacramentals and to receive the sacraments; (3) to exercise any ecclesiastical offices, ministries, functions or acts of governance" (Canon 1331, §1). An excommunication for abortion is contracted only by those who, knowing that abortion carries with it such a penalty, deliberately and willfully proceed with the abortion.

The crime of abortion, and the excommunication that goes with it, can be absolved by the Church. For such absolution the person involved must be truly repentant, must submit himself or herself to the sacrament of Penance, and must be willing to fulfill the conditions imposed by the confessor.

There are some modern Catholics who argue that all excommunications and penalties should be dropped from the Church's law, that they are incompatible with the compassion of Christ who is the Lord of the Church. Yet, at a time when abortion is so widespread and casual, this excommunication seems to me rather like the cry of the Church in the moral wilderness, pleading with its members to stop and recall what abortion really is: the deliberate destruction of innocent human life.

The excommunication emphasizes in a negative way what Pope John Paul II has declared in a positive way: "Against the pessimism and selfishness which cast a shadow over the world, the Church stands for life: In each human life she sees the splendor of that 'yes,' that 'amen,' who is Christ himself."

SOCIAL JUSTICE: IS THIS THE CHURCH'S BEST-KEPT SECRET?

Q. In one of your articles, you wrote about "certain general guidelines which flow from the social teaching of the Church. . . . '' You then went on to mention such things as the just wage, family requirements, no sexual discrimination, hospitalization insurance, pension plans, vacation time. I believe that all of these things have been beneficial to the working people of our country. But this is the first time I have heard the Catholic Church being credited with leading the way in their adoption. I had always thought of the Church as playing "catch-up football" in these areas. On what do you base your positions?

A. I base my positions on the large body of Catholic doctrine usually referred to as "Catholic Social Teaching." Every Pope since Leo XIII (1878-1903) has spoken strongly and clearly on the principles of Christian morality as they apply to economic life. Like yourself, however, many Catholics seem to be unaware of this teaching. A professor of mine used to say that "Catholic social teaching is the best-kept secret of the Church." This implies that Catholic priests and teachers do not put a high priority on teaching this material to Catholics, but it doesn't change the fact that this doctrine is an integral part of Catholic moral teaching.

The fundamental thrust of this teaching is that no area of human life, including the economic, is immune from the moral law of God. In its socioeconomic teaching, the Church tries to show how the fundamental values of justice, equity, and fairness apply to both employers and employees. In other words, the Church brings the Gospel into the marketplace.

Where does one find this material? Let me first indicate the major sources of this teaching and then offer a few practical suggestions for the average reader. The major sources are:

On the Condition of Labor (Rerum Novarum), Pope Leo XIII, 1891: Puts forward teachings by which the relations between employers and employees can be resolved in conformity with Christian principles.

Forty Years After (Quadragesimo Anno), Pope Pius XI, 1931: Reaffirms the principles of Pope Leo XIII and shows how their application should be adapted to changing times.

Christianity and Social Progress (Mater et Magistra), Pope John XXIII, 1961: Confirms and explains more fully what was taught by previous popes and sets forth the Church's teaching on new problems of the day.

The Church in the Modern World, Vatican II, 1965: Explains to all persons of good will how the Council conceives of the presence and activity of the Church in the contemporary world.

The Development of Peoples (Populorum Progressio), Pope Paul VI, 1967: Describes the worldwide dimensions of socioeconomic problems and appeals for concrete action to help all people in their full development.

On Human Work, Pope John Paul II, 1981: Reviews the socioeconomic teaching of former popes and updates many of the practical applications to fit modern realities.

In this encyclical letter of Pope John Paul II, all of the specific points you mention in your question are treated. Let me give you a few examples:

• On the just wage: "In every case a just wage is the concrete means of verifying the justice of the whole socioeconomic system and, in any case, of checking that it is functioning justly. It is not the only means of checking, but it is a particularly important one and in a sense the key means."

• On sex discrimination: "It is fitting that [women] should be able to fulfill their tasks in accordance with their own nature, without being discriminated against and without being excluded from jobs for which they are capable, but also without lack of respect for their family aspirations. . . . "

• On fringe benefits: "Besides wages, various social benefits intended to ensure the life and health of workers and their families play a part here. The expenses involved in health care, especially in the case of accidents at work, demand that medical assistance should be easily available for workers and that as far as possible it should be cheap or even free of charge. Another sector regarding benefits is the sector associated with the right to rest. In the first place this involves a regular weekly rest comprising at least Sunday and also a longer period of rest, namely the holiday or vacation. . . . A third sector concerns the right to a pension and to insurance for old age and in case of accidents at work."

Even this brief overview of the Church's teaching clearly indicates that the Church has not been playing "catch-up football" but has been involved in the game of social justice for a long time. If you would like to learn more about Catholic social teaching, I recommend that you start with the encyclical by Pope John Paul II, *On Human Work*. You will find it at any Catholic bookstore. I also recommend a fine book that digests much of the material mentioned above and presents it in a practical way: *8 Key Issues in Modern Society: A Catholic Perspective* by Mark Neilsen. (Available from Liguori Publications, Box 060, Liguori, MO 63057-9999; $2.95 plus $1.00 for postage and handling.)

IS IT WRONG TO STRIKE?

Q. During the pro football strike of 1982 I saw several reports about players who said they could not join the strike because of religious reasons or, as one said, "because I'm a Christian." Is it wrong for Christians to strike?

A. I, too, read such reports, but I had no idea which Christian church the players belonged to or why they felt as they did about strikes. In reply to your question, however, I will briefly outline the teaching of the Catholic Church on the morality of strikes.

There is no doubt that every strike (and there are about five thousand a year in the United States) brings with it some hardship. The employer loses profits, the consumer is deprived of certain goods or services, the public experiences some economic dislocation, the workers themselves suffer a loss of wages and other benefits.

It can be safely assumed, I believe, that these evils are not the direct purpose of the strike but, rather, a side effect. The main purpose, ordinarily, is the attainment of certain values or benefits that the workers feel they are entitled to, for example, better wages or improved working conditions.

Because a strike does entail the evils mentioned above, morality demands that there be sufficient proportion between the evil effects and the good. The more widespread and severe the evil effects, the more serious must be the reasons for invoking a strike. That is why many Catholic moralists believe that a strike against essential public services is hardly ever justified.

To help measure the proportion, moralists generally state that a strike may be legitimate if the following conditions are fulfilled.

1. There must be a just cause. That is, the strike must be called not out of petty feuds or rivalries but because of legitimate grievances.

2. There must be proper authorization. That is, a free and informed vote of the workers themselves (or those whom they have empowered to act in their name).

3. The strike is a last resort: that is, every other reasonable means should be exhausted before a strike is called. "The first step," as Vatican II put it, "is to engage in sincere discussion between all sides."

4. Only just means may be used: that is, work stoppage and the persuasion of other workers to support work stoppage. Strikers have no moral right to injure the person or property of the employer or other persons. Violence and force are certainly not just means.

In his 1981 encyclical, *On Human Work,* Pope John Paul II provides this excellent summary on the morality of strikes: "This method is recognized by Catholic social teaching as legitimate in the proper conditions and within just limits.

"In this connection workers should be assured the right to strike, without being subjected to personal penal sanctions for taking part in a strike. While admitting that it is a legitimate means, we must at the same time emphasize that a strike remains, in a sense, an extreme means. It must not be abused; it must not be abused especially for 'political' purposes.

"Furthermore, it must never be forgotten that, when essential community services are in question, they must in every case be ensured, if necessary by appropriate legislation."

HOW CAN GAMBLING BE JUSTIFIED?

Q. I am very upset with the Catholic churches in our town. They are forever having bingos, raffles, Las Vegas nights, and all the rest. Aren't these against the law? The Church doesn't seem to know that a lot of people get into big trouble by gambling and a lot of families are hurt by it. I don't see how gambling can be justified.

A. I certainly appreciate your feelings. I'm sure you are not the only Catholic that feels this way. It seems to me that your letter actually contains a number of questions. For the sake of clarification, I would like to separate the questions and provide a brief response to each. The questions are: Can gambling of any kind be justified? Is all gambling against the law? Should the

Church use gambling as a way to raise funds? What about compulsive or addictive gambling?

Can gambling be justified? Yes, under certain conditions. In classical moral theology gambling is considered a kind of contract. (Technically, it is referred to as an aleatory contract, from the Latin word *alea* meaning chance.) It is a contract by which the players in a game of chance agree to give the winner a certain prize or sum of money. (Bingo is a good example.) Traditionally, gambling has been considered morally justified provided the following conditions are observed: (a) the stakes belong to the one who gambles and may be freely used by him or her; (b) there is no fraud or deceit involved, such as marked cards, loaded dice, collusion with the operator; (c) there is equal risk and equal opportunity for all; and (d) there is no just prohibition by the civil authorities. When all of these conditions are fulfilled, I see no reason why gambling should be considered immoral.

Is all gambling against the law? You imply that all gambling is illegal. That is not true. In some states or counties it is legal, in others illegal. In the state where I live, for example, bingo is legal under certain conditions. In other states different forms of gambling are permitted, usually under carefully stated conditions. If in a given location gambling is, in fact, illegal, I see no justification for the Church sponsoring it. I am not naïve; I know that sometimes the Church is involved in sponsoring illegal gambling. This seems to be contrary to one of the conditions for the moral justification for gambling. Indirectly, too, it plays into the hands of the ''gangster elements'' who control so much of illegal gambling.

Should the Church use gambling as a way to raise funds? Where gambling is legal and when the other conditions are met, some priests and lay people say yes, mainly because people are attracted to this form of recreation and will respond to it. It has a good track record, they say, and you can't argue with success! As one who has served as pastor of a parish, I can relate to what they are saying. But more and more bishops, priests, and lay people seem to be saying no. The sponsorship of gambling, at the very least, gives the Church a bad image. More importantly, however, it is a poor substitute for authentic Christian stewardship. The works of the Lord in the Church should be funded by the generous giving of his people. Gambling is no substitute for that. Programs of education and formation in total stewardship are gaining momentum in the Catholic community. When they are successful, they effectively get Church organizations out of the gambling business. I, for one, have come to believe that that is the only way to go!

What about compulsive or addictive gambling? The point you make about families suffering because of excessive gambling is all too true. It has become clear that compulsive gambling is a real menace in our society. Some months ago I conducted an interview with Monsignor Joseph A. Dunne, president of the National Council on Compulsive Gambling (*Liguorian,* October 1982). This expert describes compulsive gambling as "a progressive behavior disorder in which an individual has a psychologically uncontrollable preoccupation and urge to gamble. . . . The gambling reaches the point at which it compromises, disrupts or destroys the gambler's personal life, family relationships or vocational pursuits." It is easy to see a certain resemblance between compulsive gambling and alcoholism or drug addiction. Monsignor Dunne points out, however, that compulsive gambling is easier to hide because there are no visible, external signs of it. "The compulsive gambler suffers from a serious disease, and because of the nature of that disease it is likely that the sickness will not be discovered until it is in its advanced stages."

Monsignor Dunne emphasizes, too, that compulsive gambling is much more common than the average person would suspect. "It is difficult to determine the exact number of compulsive gamblers. Some authorities estimate that there are between six and eight million compulsive gamblers in the United States. It is sometimes said that ten percent of the total population may be affected. . . . Each compulsive gambler affects ten to twelve other people:

family, friends, employers, fellow workers, and the like. . . . It is a very large problem in our society.''

Fortunately, there are signs of help on the horizon. The most effective method of dealing with compulsive gambling is through the therapy of Gamblers Anonymous, a self-help organization modeled along the lines of Alcoholics Anonymous. It now has some three hundred chapters in the United States. In it the compulsive gambler is able to compare his or her experiences with those of other gamblers, form a more positive attitude about overcoming this destructive habit, and gain support in his or her efforts. Gamblers Anonymous has two related organizations for families: Gam-Anon for spouses of compulsive gamblers and Gam-A-Teen for their teenage children. For more information, one may contact: National Council on Compulsive Gambling, Inc., 99 Park Avenue, New York, NY 10016; or Gamblers Anonymous, P.O. Box 17173, Los Angeles, CA 90017.

I would like to bring this response to a close by quoting Monsignor Dunne's wise advice for the ordinary person: "First of all, we should develop a healthy respect for those individuals and religious groups who do not wish to gamble in any shape or form. Second, we should avoid illegal gambling of any kind, even a small bet on some race or game. Each unlawful bet undermines in a small way the delicate fabric of respect for the law. Third, if someone you know seems to have fallen into the habit of compulsive gambling, try to seek help for him or her by contacting the National Council or Gamblers Anonymous.''

SHOULD THE BISHOPS TALK POLITICS?

Q. I cannot understand why the American bishops have so much to say on nuclear weapons and defense policies. Why would they talk about such topics? They are not experts. I think the bishops should tell their people to pray and keep their hands out of politics.

A. Your viewpoint is almost as old as the Church itself. During the Enlightenment — that intense period of anti-religion and anti-clericalism of the eighteenth century — some Europeans used to express it very concretely: The Church belongs in the sacristy, they said, not in the marketplace! This view reveals, I believe, a serious misunderstanding about religion and morality. This attitude, as Cardinal Bernardin has written, "divorces religion from behavior. It assumes that Christ's message holds good on Sunday but not the other six days of the week. It accepts the idea that public life not only can but should be conducted without reference to moral values, and that those who seek to evaluate public issues by the standards of morality should be shouted down and silenced."

It is certainly true that some political, economic, and military matters are almost entirely technical. Only a person who has studied those matters in a serious way is equipped to speak about them. It is safe to say that the bishops do not ordinarily possess such technical expertise.

But intertwined with almost every political, economic, and military matter is a moral question. Here the bishops have the right and the responsibility to speak out. Pope John Paul II has frequently cautioned clerics to avoid partisan politics; but, at the same time, he has urged them to speak out on the dignity of the human person, the inviolability of innocent human life, the fundamental rights of men and women given not by the State but by God himself. The Pope has emphasized that there are certain points where political and moral questions meet. The very mission of the Church demands that it address these moral questions in the light of the Gospel.

Certainly there are profound moral questions bound up in the burning issue of nuclear war. Who can deny that there are fundamental human values at stake? The possession, use, and proliferation of nuclear weapons pose some of the most difficult moral questions now facing the human race. The bishops, according to Catholic theology, are moral teachers and spiritual guides. If they don't speak out, who will? Their pastoral letter on peace and war, *The Challenge of Peace: God's Promise and Our Response* (May 1983), is aimed precisely at the formation of Christian conscience.

In their letter the bishops themselves give a clear answer to the questions you have raised: "In developing educational programs, we must keep in mind that questions of war and peace have a profoundly moral dimension which responsible Christians cannot ignore. They are questions of life and death. True, they also have a political dimension because they are embedded in public policy. But the fact that they are also political is no excuse for denying the Church's obligation to provide its members with the help they need in forming their consciences. We must learn together how to make correct and responsible moral judgments. We reject, therefore, criticism of the Church's concern with these issues on the ground that it 'should not become involved in politics.' We are called to move from discussion to witness and action" (281).

IS THERE A NEW LAW ABOUT FAST AND ABSTINENCE?

Q. A woman I work with said that Catholics are once again supposed to fast and abstain from meat on Fridays. My first reaction was "Here we go again!" Is my friend right? Is this a new law? Why can't the Church make up its mind?

A. I'm sure your co-worker was referring to a request made by the American bishops in their pastoral letter on war and peace, *The Challenge of Peace: God's Promise and Our Response*, May 1983. The fourth major section of that letter is addressed in a special way to the members of the Church and asks that we all get involved in the quest for peace. The bishops suggest four ways that the average Christian can do this. Let me say a word about each.

First, they encourage "every diocese and parish to implement balanced and objective educational programs to help people at all levels to understand better the issues of war and peace" (281). Each Catholic is encouraged to attend these programs, to read the pastoral letter in its entirety, and to arrive at a mature formation of conscience.

Second, the bishops ask all of us to recommit ourselves to a profound reverence for human life, especially that of the defenseless unborn. While acknowledging "the differences involved in the taking of human life in warfare and the taking of human life through abortion" (286), the bishops nevertheless express deep concern that society's callous attitude toward the unborn might spill over to other defenseless people as well. With penetrating insight, they remark: "We must ask how long a nation willing to extend a constitutional guarantee to the 'right' to kill defenseless human beings by abortion is likely to refrain from adopting strategic warfare policies deliberately designed to kill millions of defenseless human beings, if adopting them should come to seem 'expedient' " (288).

Third, the bishops encourage us to give a high priority to continuing prayer for peace, "for it is in prayer that we encounter Jesus, who is our peace, and learn from him the way to peace" (290). Especially emphasized are the celebration of the Eucharistic liturgy, where as a people we plead for peace and exchange the sign of peace, and prayer to Mary, the Queen of Peace.

Finally, there is an urgent plea for penance. "Prayer by itself is incomplete without penance. Penance directs us toward our goal of putting on the attitudes of Jesus himself. Because we are all capable of violence, we are never totally conformed to Christ and are always in need of conversion . . . " (297). It is at this point that the bishops make their request about fast and abstinence on Friday.

"As a tangible sign of our need and desire to do penance we, for the cause of peace, commit ourselves to fast and abstinence on each Friday of the year. We call upon our people voluntarily to do penance on Friday by eating less food and by abstaining from meat. This return to a traditional practice of penance, once well observed in the U.S. Church, should be accompanied by works of charity and service toward our neighbors. Every Friday should be a day significantly devoted to prayer, penance and almsgiving for peace'' (298).

It's clear that there is no new Church law involved here but, rather, a sincere request on the part of our bishops. There is no strict obligation to fast and abstain on Friday nor is there any sin involved if we do not do so. This is simply a positive and practical way for us to do penance ''for the cause of peace.''

IV. QUESTIONS ABOUT SEX, LOVE, MARRIAGE

**Why Is the Church So Strict
  About Premarital Sex?**
**How Should One Handle
  a Destructive Relationship?**
Sex in Marriage: Is There a Double Standard?
Can There Be Lust in Marriage?
Impotence and Sterility: Is There a Difference?
What Is an Annulment?

WHY IS THE CHURCH SO STRICT ABOUT PREMARITAL SEX?

Q. In a recent letter, Father Lowery answered a question about premarital sex. I think he was too strict. Young people look for bread and are given a stone. Doesn't he know that such teaching is driving young people away from the Church?

A. I can honestly say that the last thing in the world I would want to do is drive young people away from the Church. I do not believe, however, that I am excessively "strict" about premarital sex. Perhaps a few words of clarification will be enlightening.

Let's pause for a second and consider: When people write to me about sex, what are they actually expecting? Are they asking merely for my personal insights and observations? I doubt it. They are writing to ask about the teaching of the Catholic Church — what it is and the reasons for it. That is what I try to give them: the teaching of the Church. If I present that teaching incorrectly, I would certainly want to hear about it. But to say that "my teaching" is too strict is to miss the point. It's not my teaching but the Church's.

The teaching of the Church has been stated many times in the course of history. I know of no time when the Church said that premarital sex is a morally acceptable way for Christians to act. Some of the recent formulations of the teaching would be as follows.

— Pope John Paul II, 1981: "Consequently, sexuality, by means of which man and woman give themselves to one another through the acts which are proper and exclusive to spouses, is by no means something purely biological, but concerns the innermost being of the human person as such. It is realized in a truly human way only if it is an integral part of the love by which a man and a woman commit themselves totally to one another until death" (*On the Family,* 11).

— The Sacred Congregation for the Doctrine of the Faith, 1975: "Today there are many who vindicate the right to sexual union before marriage, at least in those cases where a firm intention to marry and an affection which is already in some way conjugal in the psychology of the subjects require this completion, which they judge to be connatural. . . . This opinion is contrary to Christian doctrine, which states that every genital act must be within the framework of marriage. . . . This is what the Church has always understood and taught, and she finds a profound agreement with her doctrine in men's reflection and in the lessons of history" (*Declaration on Certain Questions Concerning Sexual Ethics,* 1975).

— The National Conference of Catholic Bishops, 1976: "Our Christian tradition holds the sexual union between husband and wife in high honor, regarding it as a special expression of their covenanted love which mirrors God's love for His people and Christ's love for the Church. But like many things human, sex is ambivalent. It can be either creative or destructive. Sexual intercourse is a moral and human good only within marriage; outside marriage it is wrong" (*To Live in Christ Jesus*, p. 19).

Nothing I have written is "stricter" than this teaching. I have simply presented this teaching to young Catholics. To do less would be to deceive them. They have a right to know, and want to know, what the Catholic Church teaches.

At the same time, I know that young people are under heavy pressure to accept a view that is quite different from the Church's. This view comes from the general culture, from the media (especially TV and movies), and from one's peers. I sympathize with young people. I know that often enough their behavior flows from confusion and weakness rather than from malice or hardness of heart. I certainly do not intend to hand them a stone when they ask for bread. My message to them is one of encouragement. As expressed elsewhere, it is this: "The virtue of chastity is proposed to us by a Church, a community, which has been a faithful guide to men and women for nearly two thousand years. That Church, reflecting the spirit of Christ, tells us that chastity is possible and in the long run the best teacher of the complex language of sexuality and love. It reminds us, moreover, that chastity is a gift of the Holy Spirit who stands ready to give that gift to all who truly desire it" (*Following Christ: A Handbook of Catholic Moral Teaching*, pages 128-129).

HOW SHOULD ONE HANDLE A DESTRUCTIVE RELATIONSHIP?

Q. My husband and I were divorced a year ago. With the help of my pastor, I have also submitted my request for a Church annulment. Our marriage was a disaster from the start. But that is not why I am writing. I have become involved with another man. I care for him very much, and I know he cares for me. Our relationship is growing more and more intimate. But we are extremely mismatched. There is no way we should ever get married. Besides, I need some room to find myself. I want to break off with this man, but I'm afraid of the pain and hurt I will feel. Please advise.

A. There is no magic wand that can wave away the pain you will have to endure, no capsule you can take three times a day to solve your problem. The pain may get worse before it gets better, and solving this problem will demand much of you.

The advice I'm going to offer you is not taken from a modern manual of psychology but from the writings of a great saint who died almost two hundred years ago: Saint Alphonsus Liguori. This holy man was an experienced spiritual director, guiding people of every walk of life. His advice, condensed here into five basic steps, has helped many people on the pilgrimage of life. I hope it helps you.

Step 1: Conviction

You have to be deeply convinced that this relationship must be broken off. It is a dead-end relationship for both of you. You need a time for healing and growing. This relationship is crowding you. In some matters of life, a halfhearted conviction is enough for getting by. But not in the affairs of the heart. Emotional attachments between a man and a woman have strong (if not always deep) roots. If your conviction is only halfhearted, forget it. It won't work.

I encourage you to take some time in the presence of God to deepen your conviction. Pray for true wisdom to see what is right for you and for the other person. Look at the matter as honestly as you can. Then form a resolution something like this: ''Before God I am convinced that I should break off this relationship. With his grace I resolve to do so.''

Step 2: Confidence

Your conviction will not last long unless you are also confident that you can be successful. Of all the pitfalls in the moral life, perhaps the easiest to fall into is the pitfall of fatalism: ''No use trying. I'll probably start out big and fall on my face." The battle is lost before it has begun.

You can surely draw confidence from your faith. "Do not let your hearts be troubled," Jesus said. "Have faith in God and faith in me" (John 14:1). You may remember Saint Paul telling about his struggles and how he pleaded with the Lord for help. The Lord answered him, "Through the Spirit one receives faith; by the same Spirit another is given the gift of healing, and still another miraculous powers" (1 Corinthians 12:9-10). The Lord's grace is enough for you, too. In addition, you can draw confidence from the example of other Christians. Many have faced the problem you face. And many have tasted success and experienced new freedom.

Step 3: Physical Separation

If you are convinced that this relationship must end, the sooner you start ending it the better! Physical separation is a must: no more dates, no more visits, no more phone conversations. The subtle temptation is to believe that separation can be done gradually. People say, "Well, we won't see each other quite so often" or "No heavy dates, but a friendly visit for a short time won't hurt." This is like trying to quit smoking without actually quitting.

Physical presence weakens one's convictions, dilutes one's confidence, confuses one's resolution. If you don't start with physical separation, you won't start.

Step 4: Mental Separation

This means that you must control your thoughts, imagination, fantasies. Reading old love letters, reliving special moments, imagining what was or could have been — all of these simply make it harder and land you back where you started.

It is true, of course, that we don't have absolute control over our imagination and fantasies. We find that we have an all-day movie in our heads that can play tricks on us. But if we are aware of our fantasies, we can "change the image." We can gain a certain measure of control.

Step 5: Other Interests

If you physically and mentally separate from this person, you are going to have empty spaces in your heart and empty hours in your life. It will do no good to sit around wringing your hands and telling yourself how miserable you are.

The constructive thing to do is to fill the emptiness with new interests, new commitments, new friends — or even better, old friends with whom you can relax and be yourself.

What all this amounts to is that you are involved in a "freedom struggle." Freedom is never easily won. But it is worth the struggle. Saint Alphonsus once said that the power of God's grace can break any and all of the chains that keep us in slavery. May the power of his grace be with you as you move from slavery to freedom!

SEX IN MARRIAGE: IS THERE A DOUBLE STANDARD?

Q. I do not trust anything written by celibates on marriage. In your articles you idealize the woman and fail to see how unjust women can be in marriage relations. Most women use sex (or withhold sex) to manipulate their husbands. Apparently, priests are not comfortable telling wives that they too have moral obligations in the sexual structure of marriage. As it is, sex is a one-way street, completely controlled by the wife.

A. I am not sure which articles of mine you may be referring to. I freely admit that I am not an expert on the sexual relations of marriage. I do not admit, however, that I close my eyes to injustice on the part of women. Nor do I accept the sexist stereotype which you have set up: "Most women use sex (or withhold sex) to manipulate their husbands." Manipulation can be a two-way street.

I feel quite comfortable in explaining to both wives and husbands the Christian tradition of mutual sexual responsibility in marriage. This tradition is summarized in Saint Paul's first letter to the Corinthians. It has been filled out and applied by the Church's theologians in the course of time. It applies equally to men and women.

Saint Paul writes: "The husband should fulfill his conjugal obligations toward his wife, the wife hers toward her husband. A wife does not belong to herself but to her husband; equally, a husband does not belong to himself but to his wife. Do not deprive one another, unless perhaps by mutual consent for a time, to devote yourselves to prayer. Then return to one another, that Satan may not tempt you through your lack of self-control" (1 Corinthians 7:3-5).

Without attempting a thorough analysis of this text and its context, we can readily see that Paul considers marriage a natural contract in which husbands and wives freely exchange certain rights. One of these rights is the right to sexual intercourse. In classical moral theology this is called "the marriage debt"; we are talking here about the virtue of justice — what is due to each spouse — as it applies to the sexual relations of marriage.

The moral principle governing the marriage debt is: "Do not deprive one another." It has always been understood that there can be good reasons why either spouse may justly refuse sexual intercourse at a given time. (Paul mentions a spiritual reason, but there can be others as well.) Here loving sensitivity, honest communication, and "mutual consent" are obviously called for. Purely arbitrary refusal, on the other hand, has always been considered an unjust way of acting in marriage. When it becomes chronic, such refusal can not only endanger the chastity of the rejected spouse but can also erode the very foundation of the marriage.

I am very well aware that some readers will think of this approach as too legalistic for the loving relationship of sexual intercourse in Christian marriage. Saint Paul certainly does not limit his view of Christian marriage to contractual relations. (See, for example, his profoundly religious description of Christian marriage as symbolic of the love relationship between Christ and the Church in Ephesians 5:22-33.) But experience testifies that spouses can easily be tempted to use sexual intercourse for unworthy motives. Justice is the virtue that calls them to their objective, other-centered responsibilities and obligations. Justice is by no means the dominant virtue in Christian marriage, but it is an important one and certainly has its place.

CAN THERE BE LUST IN MARRIAGE?

Q. I'd appreciate your comment on our Holy Father's much debated statement about the possibility of violating marital chastity through a lack of "chastity of the heart." At times, a couple can focus primarily on expressing mutual affection; at others, the focus seems to be on relieving sexual tension. Is the latter sinful?

A. In 1980 Pope John Paul II gave a weekly homily on aspects of sexuality, marriage, and family in the teaching of Scripture and in the tradition of the Church. All of these homilies bear the stamp of the Pope's profound "personalist" philosophy and theology. In all of his major speeches and letters, you will find that he places heavy emphasis on the whole human person, body and spirit, as the receiver of God's living Word and as the center of all ethical and moral behavior. The person is paramount!

The particular statement you refer to is an example of that emphasis. At the time, even the daily papers reported this item, sometimes with a slight smirk, almost implying "How far out of it can a pope be?" Yet, it is certainly clear that the spouses in marriage do not give up their individual personhood. The man and the woman remain separate and unique persons. They retain all of their human dignity and human rights.

Pope John Paul II said that lust — the abuse of a person in the sexual sphere — can exist between husband and wife. (No counselor of any experience would deny it!) The basic teaching is that a husband can commit lust "if he treats his wife only as an object to satisfy his own instinctive needs." The same may be said of the wife in reference to her husband. The Pope's fundamental moral principle may be stated as follows: When one spouse excludes the welfare of the other and uses him or her as an object for one's own sake, lust is present in the relationship.

Nothing in the Pope's teaching condemns the relieving of sexual tension as part of the conjugal act. What he opposes (and this applies to other areas of life as well as sex) is using another person as an object of one's own satisfaction. Couples who lovingly and respectfully seek mutual affection and mutual satisfaction in the conjugal act need not worry about lust in their relationship.

IMPOTENCE AND STERILITY: IS THERE A DIFFERENCE?

Q. The Church is inconsistent in its approach to marriage. It allows the marriage of an older couple where the woman is sterile because of age, but refuses to recognize the marriage of young people if one of the partners is known to be sterile. What is the reason for this?

A. Your statement of the Church's teaching is not accurate. That is understandable because we are dealing here with complex matters. I am going to try to explain what the Church teaches in a simple, nontechnical way. I hope it is of help to you.

First, we must distinguish between *sterility* and *impotence*. In simple terms, sterility means the inability to generate children because of some physical defect. Those who are sterile are able, however, to perform the act of sexual intercourse. Impotence, on the other hand, is the inability to perform the act of sexual intercourse. Impotence is called *antecedent* impotence when it existed before the marriage. Impotence is called *perpetual* when it cannot be corrected without serious danger to life or health.

What is the Church's teaching about sterility? It is stated this way in the new Code of Canon Law: "Sterility neither forbids nor invalidates marriage" (Canon 1084, §3). Notice that this is an absolute statement and does not distinguish between young and old. Your statement that the Church allows the marriage of an older couple but refuses to recognize the marriage of young people if one of the partners is known to be sterile is not correct.

What is the Church's teaching about impotence? It too is stated in the new Code of Canon Law: "Antecedent and perpetual impotence to have sexual intercourse, whether on the part of the man or on that of the woman, whether absolute or relative, by its very nature invalidates marriage" (Canon 1084, §1).

Many people find this latter teaching difficult to understand. As long as both parties know about the impotence and are willing to accept it, they say, why would the Church consider their marriage invalid? The basic reason is that the very nature of marriage — its inner meaning by force of natural law — involves a contract by which the two parties give to each other the right of sexual intercourse. When one is incapable of sexual intercourse, one cannot enter into marriage. Other relationships, involving friendship and mutual support, are clearly possible, but not the unique relationship of marriage.

WHAT IS AN ANNULMENT?

Q. Not long ago I saw a report on TV concerning Church annulments. The wife said she did not want the annulment, but the husband did. She said, for one thing, that the annulment would mean that the children were illegitimate. The husband said he was too immature when he got married and that he really didn't understand what his marriage vows meant. What exactly is an annulment anyway?

A. Let me begin my response to your question by recalling the basic teaching of the Catholic Church on marriage. When a baptized man and a baptized woman, who are free to marry, exchange their marriage vows before an authorized priest or deacon and two witnesses and then consummate their union, their marriage is a true sacramental marriage. The sacramental bond is unbreakable; it cannot be dissolved by any power on earth, including the Church itself.

To enter into such a marriage, however, the couple must be able and willing to give their free and informed consent. Vatican II puts it this way: "The intimate partnership of life and love which constitutes the married state has been established by the creator and endowed by him with its own proper laws: it is rooted in the contract of the partners, that is, in their irrevocable personal consent" (*Church in the Modern World,* 48).

The new Code of Canon Law strongly emphasizes the role of consent in marriage: "A marriage is brought into being by the lawfully manifested consent of persons who are legally capable. This consent cannot be supplied by any human power. Matrimonial consent is an act of the will by which a man and a woman by an irrevocable covenant mutually give and accept one another for the purpose of establishing a marriage" (Canon 1057, §1 and 2).

Let us now suppose that a couple who was married in the Catholic Church runs into serious difficulties in their marriage. The difficulties persist. The marriage "breaks down." The couple finally gets a civil divorce. In the course of time, one of the spouses, or both, may wish to enter into a new marriage. The individual desires to retain full, active participation in the Church. At this point, he or she will often approach the parish priest about the possibility of an annulment of the first marriage.

An annulment is a declaration by the Church that, although there was a legal marriage in accord with state law, there was never a valid sacramental marriage in this particular case. The Church arrives at this decision only after careful and objective investigation. This investigation is carried out, under the authority of the bishop, by the marriage tribunal of the diocese.

The annulment investigation seeks to discover whether an essential ingredient for a valid sacramental marriage was lacking in this case and, if so, whether there is solid external evidence to prove this. For example, true freedom is obviously an essential ingredient for matrimonial consent. If a person were to marry while under grave fear or the threat of force ("shotgun wedding"), it is doubtful that the marriage would be valid. If one person entered marriage with the explicit intention to exclude permanence or faithfulness or the right to have children, this person would certainly be excluding an essential ingredient of marriage as understood by the Church. Or it may be that one of the parties entered the marriage suffering from a serious mental illness or "from a grave lack of discretionary judgment concerning the essential matrimonial rights to be mutually given and accepted" or from a true psychic incapacity to fulfill the essential responsibilities of marriage (see Canon 1095). In all these examples, an essential ingredient of marriage is lacking.

These are just a few examples that illustrate some of the grounds for an annulment. The task of the marriage tribunal is to examine the reasons in each case, to gather testimony from various sources, to weigh the evidence. After thorough investigation, a decision to declare the marriage valid or invalid is finally made.

I want to emphasize that an ecclesiastical annulment does not render the children illegitimate nor does it alter any civil effects of divorce, such as child support, alimony, visitation rights. The civil marriage and the civil divorce are not really affected by the annulment. The ecclesiastical annulment declares that there was not a valid sacramental marriage in this case and that, therefore, the Catholic parties are not bound to it.

SELECTED BIBLIOGRAPHY

For further reading in some of the areas covered in this booklet, I recommend the following from Liguori Publications:

THE CASE AGAINST ABORTION
A Logical Argument for Life
by Lori Van Widen — $4.95

HANDBOOK FOR TODAY'S CATHOLIC
Beliefs, Practices, Prayer
A Redemptorist Pastoral Publication — $1.95

HELPS FOR THE SCRUPULOUS
by Russell M. Abata, C.SS.R. — $4.95

HOW TO FORGIVE YOURSELF AND OTHERS
Steps to Reconciliation
(Updated and Revised)
by Reverend Eamon Tobin — $3.95

HOW THE MASS CAME TO BE
From the Last Supper to Today's Eucharist
by Pierre Loret, C.SS.R. — $2.95

THE ILLUSTRATED CATECHISM
Catholic Belief in Words and Pictures
A Redemptorist Pastoral Publication — $7.95
Leader's Guide available — $4.95

PRAYER
A Handbook for Today's Catholic
by Reverend Eamon Tobin — $4.95

SCRIPTURE-BASED SOLUTIONS
TO HANDLING STRESS
by Pat King — $5.95

HANDBOOK FOR SPIRITUAL GROWTH
A Guide for Catholics
by Philip St. Romain — $3.95

SEX AND MARRIAGE
A Catholic Perspective
by John M. Hamrogue, C.SS.R. — $2.95

MARRIAGE
A Covenant of Seasons
by Mary van Balen Holt — $7.95

HELPS FOR THE SEPARATED AND DIVORCED
by Medard Laz — $2.95

STORY OF THE MASS
From the Last Supper to the Present Day
by Pierre Loret, C.SS.R. — $5.95

BODY MIND SPIRIT
Tapping the Healing Power Within You
A 30-Day Program
by Richard P. Johnson, Ph.D. — $6.95

PIERCING THE MIST
Glimpses of God in the Wonders of Life
by Leo Holland — $7.95

YOUR FAITH
A Popular Presentation of Catholic Belief
A Redemptorist Pastoral Publication — $7.95

(Continued on page 64.)

OTHER BOOKS BY THE SAME AUTHOR

A BASIC CATHOLIC DICTIONARY
Complete yet compact, this is a layman's dictionary of often-asked-about words and phrases. Entries come from many aspects of Church life. Approximately 450 terms and names along with a brief, easy-to-understand explanation of each. **$4.95**

DAY BY DAY THROUGH LENT
Reflections, Prayers, Practices
Rich reflections on the biblical readings for each day. Simple, heartfelt prayers and down-to-earth practices that will help you express love for God and neighbor in concrete, practical ways. **$3.95**

FOLLOWING CHRIST
A Handbook of Catholic Moral Teaching
This popular book answers the most-often-asked questions about morality and presents moral guidelines for living in today's world. Drawing from sacred Scripture and from the teachings of great theologians of the past and the present, the author takes a simple, straightforward look at the teachings of Jesus and the demands of discipleship. **$3.95**

Order from your local bookstore or write to
Liguori Publications
Box 060, Liguori, MO 63057-9999
*(Please add $1 for postage and handling for orders
under $5; $1.50 for orders over $5.)*